21st Century Basic Skills Library

BABY ZOO ANIMALS
GIRAFFES

by Josh Gregory

Cherry Lake Publishing • Ann Arbor, Michigan

3

Published in the United States of America
by Cherry Lake Publishing
Ann Arbor, Michigan
www.cherrylakepublishing.com

Content Adviser: Dr. Stephen S. Ditchkoff, Professor of Wildlife Sciences, Auburn University, Auburn, Alabama

Photo Credits: Cover and pages 1 and 10, ©Henk Bentlage/Shutterstock, Inc.; page 4, ©Julija Sapic/Shutterstock, Inc.; page 6, ©Moodville/Dreamstime.com; page 8, ©Ivan Cholakov/Dreamstime.com; page 12, ©Dolce Vita/Shutterstock, Inc.; page 14, ©Melody Revnak/Dreamstime.com; page 16, ©Roman Murushkin/Dreamstime.com; page 18, ©Juris Sturainis/Dreamstime.com; page 20, ©Dean Pennala/Dreamstime.com

Library of Congress Cataloging-in-Publication Data
Gregory, Josh.
  Giraffes / by Josh Gregory.
       p. cm. — (21st century basic skills library) (Baby zoo animals)
    Includes bibliographical references and index.
    ISBN 978-1-61080-456-1 (lib. bdg.) — ISBN 978-1-61080-543-8 (e-book) — ISBN 978-1-61080-630-5 (pbk.)
  1. Giraffe—Infancy—Juvenile literature. 2. Zoo animals—Infancy—Juvenile literature. I. Title.
  SF408.6.G57G74 2013
  599.638—dc23   2012001727

Cherry Lake Publishing would like to acknowledge the work of The Partnership for 21st Century Skills. Please visit www.21stcenturyskills.org for more information.

Printed in the United States of America
Corporate Graphics Inc.
July 2012
CLFA11

TABLE OF CONTENTS

Tall Tales

Giraffes are the tallest land animals.

Wild giraffes live in Africa.

You can also see them at zoos.

A baby giraffe is as tall as a grown person!

Giraffes have one **calf** at a time.

A mother giraffe stands up to give birth. The calf falls a long way to the ground when it is born.

This does not hurt the baby.

Giraffes have long legs, long necks, and long tongues. These help them reach food at the tops of trees.

Giraffes are covered in dark spots. Every giraffe's spots are **unique**.

A Giraffe's Day

Giraffes spend most of their time eating and relaxing.

They sleep for about 30 minutes each day. They take short naps day and night. Each nap only lasts for a few minutes.

Calves drink milk from their mothers. Adult giraffes eat leaves.

Zookeepers also feed giraffes special **biscuits**. This food keeps the giraffes healthy.

Giraffe calves and their mothers **communicate**. They like to touch and lick.

Giraffes can also hiss and roar. Sometimes they moo like a cow!

Giraffe calves stay together in groups.

Giraffe mothers help watch over each other's calves.

Reaching New Heights

Calves grow taller and stronger as they get older.

Adult giraffes are about three times as tall as an adult human.

Giraffes can have calves of their own when they are about 4 years old.

Then there is a new giraffe at the zoo!

Find Out More

BOOK

Keller, Susanna. *Meet the Giraffe*. New York: PowerKids Press,
2010.

WEB SITE

San Diego Zoo—Animal Bytes: Giraffe
www.sandiegozoo.org/animalbytes/t-giraffe.html
Watch a video and read more about giraffes.

Glossary

biscuits (BIS-kuts) small, round bread

calf (KAF) baby of certain animals, such as giraffes

communicate (kuh-MYOO-ni-kate) share information, ideas, or
feelings

giraffes (jur-AFS) very tall mammals that live in Africa

unique (yoo-NEEK) not like anything else, different

zookeepers (ZOO-kee-purz) workers who take care of animals
at zoos

Home and School Connection

Use this list of words from the book to help your child become a better reader. Word games and writing activities can help beginning readers reinforce literacy skills.

a	does	healthy	mother	short	three
about	drink	heights	mothers	sleep	time
adult	each	help	nap	sometimes	times
Africa	eat	hiss	naps	special	to
also	eating	human	necks	spend	together
and	every	hurt	new	spots	tongues
animals	falls	in	night	stands	tops
are	feed	is	not	stay	touch
as	few	it	of	stronger	trees
at	food	keeps	old	take	unique
baby	for	land	older	tales	up
birth	from	lasts	one	tall	watch
biscuits	get	leaves	only	taller	way
born	giraffe	legs	other's	tallest	when
calf	giraffe's	lick	over	the	wild
calves	giraffes	like	own	their	years
can	give	live	person	them	you
communicate	ground	long	reach	then	zoo
covered	groups	milk	reaching	there	zookeepers
cow	grow	minutes	relaxing	these	zoos
dark	grown	moo	roar	they	
day	have	most	see	this	

Fast Facts

Habitat: Grasslands

Range: Parts of Africa south of the Sahara Desert.

Average Height: Between 14 and 18 feet (4.3 and 5.5 meters)

Average Weight: Between 1,500 and 3,000 pounds (680 and 1,360 kilograms)

Life Span: About 15 to 20 years

Index

About the Author

Josh Gregory writes and edits books for children. He lives in Chicago, Illinois.